IMPERFECTION:
THE ONE-EYED CHILD

A Life Through Monocular Vision

CLAIRE GALE

authorHOUSE®

AuthorHouse™ UK
1663 Liberty Drive
Bloomington, IN 47403 USA
www.authorhouse.co.uk
Phone: 0800.197.4150

Published by AuthorHouse 07/14/2017

ISBN: 978-1-5246-8353-5 (sc)
ISBN: 978-1-5246-8354-2 (hc)
ISBN: 978-1-5246-8355-9 (e)

Written from diary extracts, *Imperfection: The One-Eyed Child* chronicles the journey of a courageous thirteen-year-old girl, how the traumatic event that changed her life happened, and its results. Along with the perspective contained in the diary extracts, *Imperfection* presents the feelings and insight of concerned parents.

To all the paramedics, nurses, and doctors who've helped me over the years.

The staff at Hereford County Hospital, Birmingham Children's Hospital, and all on the wards at Bristol Frenchay Hospital ICU, including the surgical ward, all of the staff who helped me throughout everything, and the nurses and doctors who were called in. And to HABIT, the head injury team that has worked closely with me.

To the Midlands Air Ambulance crew and staff who have helped me over the years since 21 November 2008. To Colin Apps, Nick Cunningham, Annie and Helen, and the other staff I have met throughout this whole journey, all of whom have helped me piece normality back together.

To Jack Sparrow (Johnny Depp) for starring in Pirates of the Caribbean *and keeping me company a fair few times a day throughout the whole of this.*

To my daughter, Chloe-Mae, my rock, my constant, my everything. You are the little thing that fills my heart and keeps me going on a daily basis, my little ray of sunshine sent to light up my life.

To my gorgeous – and not quite such a puppy now – Tom, my beautiful boy who helped me through and understood. You are sentimental to me, the piece of this puzzle I have been holding onto for the past eleven years. I owe you so much. You're a not-so-good show dog, a pet, and a counsellor; you would just lie there and listen. And no matter what, you always got it. You were always gentle around me. You were meant to be mine from day one, and even though you were sold, you still came back for me. I treasure our memories. Your loss hit me hard. It's time to let go. You may be gone, but you'll never be forgotten. You have left your mark on everyone, especially my heart. 23 May 2003 to 23 July 2014

To my mum and dad, my brother, and all those people who were there to help me fight, keep me strong, and win the battle with myself. You fought not for me but with me. And for those who are always there – no matter what.

*For you **who** captured my heart and hold the key. You have been my strength and helped me find myself when I was lost. You light me up and put a massive smile on my face. You make me feel whole. Hopefully there will be lots more happiness between us.*

And last, to the person who said to me, "You are nothing." It was a hard thing to realise that you didn't love me and never did and that it was all an act to get what you wanted. I wasted so much time believing that you actually did love me, but with this book I can say: I am something.

CONTENTS

THIS IS ME

Childhood is not from birth to a certain age, and at a certain age the child is grown, and puts away childish things. Childhood is the kingdom where nobody dies.
—Edna St Vincent Millay

Hi! My name is Claire. I'm twenty-four. I'm into art, poetry, and creative writing. I'm a wannabe model – ha! But no way do I have the figure for it! Or maybe I'm just a wannabe photographer, but I don't take criticism well.

Okay, wait. Scrap that. Here's a better insight into me. Where to start? My life has been such a mess. It's been up. It's been down. A lot.

I have never really belonged and never felt like 'me'. I don't know who I am, what I am.

Am I anything? I sure don't feel it sometimes.

So here you go; here's an insight into a messed-up young girl's life – all the trials and tribulations.

I have nothing left in the world except for the most beautiful daughter, who will always be my life jacket when I'm drowning. And hopefully, one day she will be proud of who I am.

I'm hoping for the chance of happiness, one day. I get called fat and ugly. I get told that I'm nothing.

I get called a comedian for the jokes that I crack, but they are based on events in my life, and they stop me from crying. Otherwise, the tears will just keep falling.

I write lyrics and poems to vent my hurt and anger towards those who have cussed and cursed me.

I call everyone pet names because I feel that I make them comfortable. But it only ever brings anger and war.

I question my own sanity most days, as I don't know what you want anymore. I smile and cry with laughter because, if I stop smiling, I feel like I'll crack and never come out at the other end of the tunnel.

I'm an average size, yet I look in the mirror and see a fat, ugly person. I nod at myself and smile for reassurance to make me feel better. I talk to myself because I often feel I have no one else.

I feel like a burden, a let-down, a failure – like nothing at all. I'm broken and falling apart, a bit battered around the edges and not perfect.

I hope it's not true, and I need to believe in myself more; yet I don't. I voice my opinion, and I get grief for it.

I wake up nearly every morning and wonder, *Do I have to get up to this life again?* But I must use every ounce of my being to push on through and act normal, as if nothing is questioned. I'm just purely existing.

And all the obstacles I've overcome in my life so far – I always planned my life to turn out differently. I had ideas; I had it all mapped out.

This life isn't for me but for my perfect little girl.

I feel poorly, anxious, edgy, and exhausted all the time; I don't know why.

I have nightmares about my past and the stuff that's been caused and happened. I think it'll be forever etched in my brain. I have sleepless nights, tossing and turning.

We grow up with the idea that we have to look to others for answers. Instead of seeking approval, look inside yourself, and feel what is right. We are all unique. Therefore, we are all on our own paths. Others cannot tell you exactly what to do because their destinations are different from yours.

Life isn't about how many breaths you take; it's what takes your breath away.

There are steps in everyone's life where you change from an infant to a youngster, from a teen to an adult. Seeing the before and after, I've changed quite a bit. I used to live life as a scared individual, someone who's wary and afraid to get hurt again. I sit here and think about life, and I strongly believe everyone is on a path, a journey that is mapped out for each individual. There are right and wrong turns and obstacles that may get in your way, but life is what you make it.

This is my life.

This is my path.

This is my journey.

This is what I have made of it.

Given the things I've overcome and faced, I will deal with what life throws at me and take it day by day.

I wear my heart on my sleeve all the time. And people are prone to breaking it. Everyone is so quick to judge.

I ain't nowhere near perfect. I eat when I'm bored. I fall for boys easily.

I'm hoping one day I won't have to fake a smile. I make up excuses for everything. I have best friends and enemies, but that's life.

Live it and love it! And most of all, learn from it!

Someone once said to me that people moan and whine about such trivial things, yet the person who has been through the worst possible things ever is the one who can stand up and face the world and all its negatives – and still be so positive. 'I don't know how you do it,' the person said. 'You're amazing.'

My reply was, 'I have to make a stand and face life head-on. If I don't accept it, how can I expect others to? Yeah, I was dealt a tough hand. But I want to be someone my daughter is proud of. So no matter how much I'm crumbling inside, I have to stand here and smile, repeating those three well-known words: "I am fine!"'

And things change. Your friends may leave. But remember life doesn't stop for anybody. Have you walked in my shoes? Have you lived in my head? Have you witnessed my life?

No!

So please don't that think you have or that you can begin to understand, because trust me, you won't!

Life is about chances – chances to change things and make things better; chances to change history; and chances to pick yourself up, dust yourself off, and carry on.

The girl you see pretends to keep everyone happy. I try my hardest – I do – in everything just to please people and to have an easy life.

But you know what? I'm no princess, and fairy tales don't last forever.

Okay, so let's start at the beginning. Everything happens in threes, so here is my life. I am thankful for my struggle because without it, I wouldn't have found my strength.

16 October 2003

21 November 2008

8 July 2014

16 OCTOBER 2003

Life is like a camera.
Focus on what's important. Capture the good times.
Develop from the negatives.
And if things don't work out,
take another shot.
I have not slept.
Between the acting of a dreadful thing and the first motion,
all the interim is like a phantasm or a hideous dream.

I'm a coin of Hereford, Herefordshire. I was made in the year 1990, and I've been punched from sheet metal. I've been stamped and cleaned. My edges have been rimmed and bevelled.

But now I have a hole in me. I'm no longer in perfect condition. Imperfection.

I want to tell you the story of my life so far.

I'm not the only person in this godforsaken world who has been through half this shit. I'm one person. But I can find the courage to stand up and tell my story. I can talk about being bullied, tormented, scared, alone, and hurt. I can share how I was in pain, abused, and beaten and have still stood tall and strong and ready to face whatever life throws at me next.

Hopefully, my story will give light at the end of the tunnel for other people who think they are alone. Perhaps they'll believe in themselves a bit more and know they are not on their own.

It does get better. Eventually. That's a promise.

Happily ever afters don't exist, happen, work out, or whatever. But. Everyone is given a once upon a time and the chance to write his or her own novel and get the life he or she wants.

I finally found mine. Everything happens for a reason. Paths are meant to collide and destined to meet and become one.

So there is something I want to tell you. Right before everything went black at every near-death experience I faced, you want to know the last thing that entered my mind?

You. Your dark eyes staring at me, your smile. You whispered, 'It's not your time. One day I'll give you back what's yours.' You stopped me from going too soon and kept me on my path to meet you.

You make my heart melt. Everything between us is linked, and our paths were destined to cross. It's been written in the stars for a very long time.

So for that, I thank you.

Things in life get lost. They disappear and then reappear. You lose precious things. And things you thought you'd like to keep.

The one thing that has stayed with me is the diary I kept when I was thirteen throughout the ordeal that would forever change my life – because there are no accidents in life, and everything happens for a reason.

***

Me, normal? Pfft! What is normal?

The dictionary says it's 'conforming to the standard or the common type; usual; not abnormal; regular; natural.'

Well, that's me. For a start, I'm unusual, abnormal, unregular, and everything that you're not meant to be if you're to be defined as normal. This is the day that changed my life forever. There are definitions and meanings, but does this 'normal' person actually exist? Are there people who meet that exact criteria? Well, whoever they are, I'd love to shake their hands and congratulate them on being the perfect people to fit into this society.

It was a Wednesday morning, and I had just woken up to get ready for school. I was thirteen and in my third year of secondary school. I hated getting up in the morning. It was always such a struggle to get up and leave my nice, warm bed, especially now that it was getting into winter and getting colder. I got dressed in my uniform, tied my tie, and shoved my hair up into a sassy ponytail. I grabbed all my school bits, threw them into my bag, and made sure I had everything and all my books for that day. It soon hit twenty past eight. My mum had already left for work, as she was over in Hereford and working late. She wouldn't be home till gone nine tonight.

I carried on to meet my best friend. We did everything together; we were inseparable. That included us getting lifts to school together or walking home – although the latter was rarely the case. Her Nanna was dropping us off at school today, and then my dad would be picking us up after it from the usual place round the corner from the school.

When we arrived at school, this is where we always went our separate ways to meet our other friends – our classmates – as we were in different sets and years at school. She was in her first year, and I was in my third. By the time I had met my school friends, the bell was ringing and it was time to line up for tutorial. I was in green house. We lined up by the science block. I didn't really speak to many people or have many friends. I preferred it to just be me and just kept myself to myself and got through each day. I did what I was there to do – learn.

The first lesson of the day was maths. I sat at the back of the class in the middle row. I'd just get lost in my work, so that the ninety-minute lesson passed quickly. That helped me avoid the jeering and the comments of fellow classmates. 'Squat.' 'Square.' 'Geek.' Those were just a few of the names that I regularly got called and put up with on a daily basis. Who gave them the right to label people and brand them? Who made them the gods of school? Did anyone? Or was that just their place in the society of this high school? I just wanted to do well and try to get places. Was that so hard to do? Would it be so hard to actually accomplish what I had always hoped for?

I think that's why I enjoyed my own company so much; at least if you were alone, there was no one to hurt you – that is, except yourself. There was no one to blame, no one to make you feel crumpled and worthless, as if you had no reason to be here and no purpose. If you were alone, you could do what you had to do to get through the day. That's why I preferred to be alone. It was best to be by myself.

As I snapped out of my wondering daydream, the bell rang its chime once more. It was twelve twenty-five. This bell signalled that it was lunchtime. This was when the school, at the same time everyday, turned into a zoo. Literally all the students resembled animals. They bustled around and hurried down the corridors like scavengers looking for food, following the scent of the canteen slop. They were like a stampede through the halls for lunch, people always hanging and monkeying around, people slithering along and chuckling like hyenas.

I packed up my belongings slowly and threw my bag over my shoulder. I wrapped my blazer tightly around my body, to try and hide it. I wanted to make myself invisible and to blend in, to just disappear. I kept my head down and walked swiftly down to lunch. You didn't hang around on your own too much, and at all costs, you were to avoid big gangs of people. That's when you'd run into trouble. It was especially important to avoid the older, scary-looking lads. They were like giants; they were so intimidating. They always seemed to somehow make you blush with embarrassment. If you blushed, then it got worse. And knowing my luck, they would manage to find something to say if I stuck around too much. The mantra that used to run through my head went something like this – no fast walking, without tripping or falling, and the quicker the better.

I made my way down to the small hall. There were always ten large tables out with chairs all around them. The hall was already filled with people, sitting, laughing, eating, and queuing for the food from the hatches. There at the edge of the hall was a singular table and a chair with my name on it. There were five of us all together, and we all huddled around this table out of the way of the others. I always seemed to stick out like a sore thumb, but we seemed to always manage to have a good laugh about our classes and just seemed to click. We understood how each other felt, as we were all in the same boat.

I often thought it wasn't fair. Why me? Why did I have to be the one to never fit in? I knew I was better off on my own. That's what I enjoyed. But I hated not fitting in and always being alone. I hated never having friends – at all. But it never stopped myself from questioning it:

But that's what you preferred wasn't it, Claire?

No of course not!

But does any one care?

No! Don't be so silly.

No one understands you. So why would they care?

Well, they wouldn't!

Right?

Once I'd finished my lunch, I quickly packed up and hurried off to the library I was bound to find a quiet corner in there where I could read and attempt to concentrate on my work. There could even be someone to chat with or to keep me company. Maybe I could find someone to fit in with. Did anyone like that actually exist? Or was this my destiny? Thirteen and alone? I didn't think anyone really understood what it was like to be alone, 24/7. It was the most miserable existence. No one would ever truly get that because they had never gone through it themselves. They wouldn't know what it was like to be me. If someone understood, they wouldn't leave me alone. Right?

Some days I was so down, "d secretly brush away falling tears. Why would I want to go to the one place where I was pushed down and degraded, to be around those people who would make me feel like I was nothing, like I didn't have a right to be there? Why did I force myself there to make myself better when I was obviously nothing to anyone? Would I really be a better person at the end? Would anyone be proud of me?

Wasn't that all that anyone ever wanted—for someone to be proud of them. If I were to just shrivel up and disappear or die and be removed from this life, would anyone actually notice? Would anyone remember who I was? Would people cry over my loss? Or would no one bat an eyelid. Would life just go on for everyone as it did every day? Would people struggle to remember who I was? There were a few selected teachers I was close to, along with my tutor and the librarian, and they'd always try to check that I was okay. No matter what, come rain or shine, the answer was always the same. 'I am fine.' I said it so many times I believed it myself sometimes. But what does *fine* actually mean? Whatever it was I was 100 per cent sure it wasn't anything that I was.

Did I even know how I felt anymore? Or was I fooling even myself? I probably was fooling myself those days. However, what I was meant to be was one big act; I was to be a happy little Claire, who was fine – just fine, perfectly fine, absolutely fine. No matter how often I said it, though, it never really fully described anything about how I truly felt or how I actually was.

Soon the bell rang again, meaning lunchtime was over. Thank god. Lunchtimes were just long enough. I stepped out of my own little world and back into reality.

First thing on the agenda was tuition and registration. It was the one reason I was here, the one way I knew I'd be noticed or missed. That soon finished.

English was next. This was good. It was something I felt good at, something I enjoyed. We were reading a play and making our very own children's books. I was so proud of mine, even if nobody else was. It was a short lesson, and after sixty minutes the bells rang again. I hopped up and slipped out of the class heading to my next lesson.

Fifth period on a Wednesday afternoon was art. Art I loved. I lost my self in this subject. I could just let myself go and think about nothing except my blank canvas. This lesson sped by. Art was about putting feelings down without using words. It was my way of logging my life, my journey, of piecing it all together like a collage on a blank piece of paper.

Soon we were packing up and waiting for the bell, which would announce that it was chucking out time from the zoo. You could almost guarantee a fight at the end of the day and for the idiocy and the monkeying around in this zoo to start up. I left the 'D' block and waited for my friend outside of the leisure centre.

She soon met up with me. We started speaking as soon as we met up. It was weird – like I belonged. I could be myself around her. We laughed and joked on the way back to the car and discussed tonight's plans and what would happen.

We walked around to the corner shop where my dad met me. My brother was already in the car. We both slipped into the car, continuing our conversation. We arrived at my house. She and I arranged to go out after dinner, in about an hour. She went down to hers to get ready.

I ran into the house and up into my room. I changed, putting on my brother's green hoody, my jeans, and his Vans trainers. I thought this outfit looked cool; plus, it was comfy, and it was me.

By the time I was ready, so was dinner. Dad called us down. Oven-cooked fish and chips, followed by chocolate treacle pudding. Yummy.

And shortly after, a knock sounded at the door. My friend was outside with her BMX bike, just like we had organised.

We started speaking about the puppies. We had been over recently to view the golden retriever puppies that the neighbour's dog had given birth to. They were adorable. There was one in particular that I liked. He was mine, no matter what anyone said. Tom was the palest of the whole litter. He was the quietest, but he was the one I wanted. It was destined. I just knew it. He had been sold. But something had happened with the people who'd bought him, and within twenty-four hours, he was back with the breeders. I just knew it was fate. My parents had said no every time I asked if I could have him. But I just knew he'd be mine – at some point, somehow.

We were taking it in turns – one of us riding whilst the other stood on the stunt pegs at the back. We had tried using the front ones, but this meant sitting on the handlebars, and I wasn't very good at that.

Our neighbourhood friend lived a few houses from us, in the middle between my house and the park. We stopped by to see him. He went to a different school. And he was older. He was 15. He was showing us his airgun and his little target, where he was shooting at party poppers on a string. After a few minutes, we got bored and decided to continue on to the park. It was my turn to turn the bike around.

I began peddling to the park. Within a split second, *bang.* My life would never be the same again.

I screamed. My stomach churned and pain took over my body. I jumped off the bike. Panic struck. The intense pain, numbed my brain. I couldn't see at all. I shouted, 'I think I have been shot.' The blood started pouring. My eyes were bleeding, so were my nose and my ears, and I was spitting out blood.

He jumped over the wall acting like a hero. I had my bestie on one side of me and him on the other leading me around to the front of his house. All he could say was, 'Is that your eye hanging out?' Just the boost of confidence to dull the panic that was bubbling inside of me. Instead it was made worse by the insensitive comment that was spilling out of this monster. How could he have done this? Why me? Was I really disliked that much that my own life was dealing me a duff hand and turning away from me?

I was made to stand outside whilst they discussed what to do. The blood was pouring out onto their drive, and all I kept thinking was that it looked like spaghetti hoops—with all the little tendons and goodness knows what falling out with the blood. The dizziness started to take over, and I went light-headed.

The lad's sister went to get my dad, and told him to bring something to mop me up. He grabbed the kitchen roll and came to me straight away. He took one look and said he needed more to sort this. I was given a tea towel to put over my face and led in, making sure I didn't get blood on the carpet.

I sat in their kitchen with a blood-soaked towel over my face, shaking, feeling sick, and getting distressed and panicking. And I had the worst heavy headache ever. They called an ambulance. Shortly, Dad arrived back. He had gone to get his shoes and leave my brother with my grandma, as the injury was a lot bigger than a kitchen roll mop-up job. Even I could tell that, given the pain I was in and the way my head became so heavy that I couldn't hold it up. All I wanted to do was sleep.

The first response man arrived. I had a sudden wave of tiredness take over my body. It was as if it was taking over my body and shutting me down. The numbness spread over me. I was led out to the car ambulance. I moaned. If I had to go in an ambulance, it could have been a real one, a big one.

My mate stood outside on the driveway to give the first responders room. I remember she was really upset and had begun crying. I assured her I was fine. That's all I could be. After all that had happened, I could use that phrase again – 'I'm fine – even though I knew I wasn't. What else could be said? I had to be brave.

At least I had the *nee, naahhs* and the blue flashing lights all the way to Hereford. It made the fact of not having the big ambulance a little better. But they would not hear the last of it.

We arrived in Hereford. My mother was already there, waiting for us, as Dad had already rung her. She was on reception at work. He had told her that I had been shot and that it was bad – really bad. Her face dropped after answering the phone at work. Her whole world crashed in around her. Was I okay? Was I going to be okay?

Someone brought me a wheelchair so I could be taken in. I wasn't allowed to walk. I had to keep still. Goodness knows what I looked like. I got wheeled in and seen immediately. I had a fan group it looked like waiting for me. They bustled around, putting in cannulas and drips, administrating pain relief, and organising scans and tests to be done to check the extent of the damage. The hospital had to call the specialist in from home. Was this it? Had I finally been noticed?

That night was about to be the longest night of my little life – a changing life, a life that had been forced to change. This was the first night of hell. This was the first night of my new life.

MAGGIE FELLOWS

Bless a thing and it will bless you.
Curse it and it will curse you.
If you bless a situation, it has no power to hurt
you, and even if it is troublesome for a time, it will
gradually fade out, if you sincerely bless it.
The three C's of life –
Choices. Chances. Changes.
You must make a choice to take a chance
or your life will never change.
Life lesson #2: No one makes a lock without a key. That's
why god won't give you problems without solutions.
Pain is never permanent.

I was surrounded and overwhelmed with all the hustle and hurrying of the on-call doctors and nurses. Everyone was rushing to do things to care for me. I knew it was going to be a long night, and I knew it was going to be longer every moment something was drawn out, and it uncovered something else.

It started to be a haze, but the pain was surreal. My head had become so heavy. I couldn't lift it. Was it even my head? Because it was heavy to move, it didn't feel as if it was attached to my body. Maybe this was all a dream. Maybe I was dreaming so much my subconscious had taken over, making my dream lifelike. It was too real for comfort.

I had people poking and prodding me, sticking needles in my arms and the back of my hands. And they were always whispering; they were all whispering about something – something that was me. What was so important that I had to be kept out of the loop? That I wasn't to know? Was I dead? Dying? Was it really that serious?

I was connected to a drip. 'Nil by mouth' was written by my name. No food or drink – just in case surgery was on the cards. But nothing as yet was set in stone, not until they had test results or scan pictures. I was on major painkillers though. They were numbing my body, numbing the pain, and Leaving this fire of pain simmering in the back of my mind. No matter what, my head remained heavy, so heavy it couldn't be moved.

I kept being wheeled down to different places – to have my scans and different tests, to find out what damage had been done, and to makes sure that it wasn't too much and that the pellet had actually stopped travelling. Wherever it had gone or was going.

When I got back to the A & E department cubicle, they announced that it was touch-and-go and that they couldn't be certain if the pellet had stopped. They didn't know what to do. They called the primary eye specialist in from home. He came to check the situation out, to discover what was up with it, and to help determine what the next steps would be.

I'd be okay. I was fine. I always was. This was the easy way out of being invisible. I never took the easy way. I liked a challenge. Adventure was always worthwhile. Right?

The feeling of the painkillers was cold in the back of my hand. It numbed my body, tingling through my veins. It was bubbling way down in my stomach, along with my fish and chips. I started being violently sick. I could hardly sit up, and I couldn't move. I felt like a robot, like I was an unmovable figure that wasn't meant to pose in a different position. My mum never left my side. My dad went home to get some overnight bits. The nurse got Mum to clean me up; she said that she didn't do sick. I remember being changed and having new blankets laid over me. I remember always being made comfortable. Was this it? Was this what they did when they didn't know how long was left?

Is this what the walk to death felt like? Was this leading up to it? People fluffing pillows? Doting on you? Making sure you're comfortable. I was fine. I was screaming out that I was fine. No one was listening. I didn't know if they could actually hear me. I was a mute. I was screaming out, yet no sound was coming out of me. All I wanted to do was to get up and go. I was restricted. I had invisible chains pinning me to the bed. This time, I couldn't break free.

I had a nurse who never left my side too. She was always there. I think because I was young, the hospital staff felt for me. They knew the possible outcomes and what might be. Death. I hurt thinking about it. Could I leave my loved ones behind? Imagine the pain that surrounded this. And my bubble was now enclosing so many people who were so close to me. If this bubble were to be popped, everyone else's world inside it would also come crashing down. I couldn't do that. I couldn't let that be the case, I couldn't watch on from the afterlife, watching all their lives come crashing down around their feet, where they wouldn't be able to stop it. Unstoppable forces were in a play – something that couldn't be changed had begun, something that had already been set into motion. It was the thing that I had to fight against, no matter how weak I was.

The doctor who had been summoned from home arrived shortly. He was briefed outside the room and told all about my case. Maybe they went outside so as to not scare me. It didn't work. I had never been so scared in my life. I was fighting back tears – tears of fear, tears of pain, and tears of not actually knowing what might happen.

Just keep smiling, Claire. You're fine. Just remember that.

He soon came to see me and to take a look at the damage. He took one look at me and my eye, shining a light into it, and stood straight back. He turned to the nurse and apologised. His words were, 'I'm so sorry. This is out of my hands. Transfer her straight to Birmingham Children's. The lead pellet is still travelling through her brain.'

As soon as these words left his lips, the nurse left the room to contact the ambulance drivers, who would escort me with blue lights, immediately, to Birmingham Children's Hospital.

Maggie Fellows was the name of the nurse who never left me. She wanted to come with me to Birmingham in the ambulance, to hold my hand. I couldn't have a parent because I was too ill. I needed a nurse and two paramedics to travel with me. I owe her everything for the support and the care she gave me that night.

The paramedics didn't take long to arrive, and soon they were introducing themselves to me. My mum and dad said they would see me in Birmingham and that they loved me. I will never know how they did it. I can only imagine the pain they must have felt, saying goodbye to their daughter and not knowing if it would be the last time.

I felt the silent tears emerging. I fought so hard to keep them back. I had to be brave. If I broke down or started crying, people would know I was scared – would know how scared I actually was. I would rather them remember me as being a brave little girl if that's how things were to turn out. I was going to hold everyone else up around me, support all of them. Tears weren't going to help this situation. They were not going to make it any easier or better. And they weren't going to make it go away. What was done was done. I was going to face it head-on like a brave young girl.

I was moved from the one bed to the other. Moving my head triggered the pain all off again. The pain washed throughout my entire body, like an electric current. Another wave of exhaustion swept through my body. I was wheeled out of the hospital. It wasn't the escape plan I was planning on. It was so cold. The wind sent a shiver down my spine. I was put into the back of the ambulance. My mum and dad said goodbye and reassured me that they would meet me at the hospital. They hurried to their car to follow the ambulance. I'd never lain down in bed in the back of a moving vehicle before. It was so fast. All you could see were lights whizzing past the smoked-out window in the back of the vehicle. Suddenly, that bubbling feeling was back in my stomach. The sickness was back with a vengeance.

The nurse kept trying to speak to me, making sure I was okay and that I wasn't in any pain. She kept checking my blood pressure and making sure I was okay. I was exhausted, though. I just wanted to close my eyes. My body was trying to shut down.

All I kept thinking about was everyone else. Were they okay? Was my best friend all right? And was my brother okay?

At the bottom of it all, I knew that I was sick. But it wasn't myself I was worried about or who I thought about too much. It was everyone else that was now worrying about me. No one was meant to worry about me. If everyone else feared the worst and was worried, how could I stay strong and grin and bear it?

The sickness subsided a little. We soon arrived in Birmingham. The ambulance never slowed, rarely stopping. We arrived at the Birmingham Children's Hospital by 11.30 p.m. The ambulance pulled up outside, and the paramedics began to unload me. There were nurses already there waiting for my big entrance, for my arrival, just like I was royalty.

The hospital looked like a maze with its different doors, lifts, and twists and turns. The medical people were talking as they walked taking me up to the ward.

When I arrived there, I was tagged with yet another number. I was one of many sick children in this hospital. Little did I know this was all preparing me for round two of the prodding and probing, followed by more tests and scans.

Mum and Dad arrived shortly after I did, and they came with me for the tests. These were going to determine my fate. What would become of me? It would all be fine. I just knew it. I kept thinking it all had to be all right. Right?

C-747414

When life gives you a hundred reasons to cry, show
life that you have a thousand reasons to smile.
Take a chance and never let go.
Risk everything, loose nothing.
Don't worry about anything anymore.
Cry in the rain and speak up loud.
Say what you want and love who you want.
Be yourself and not what people want to see.
Never blame anyone if you get hurt.

You took the risk, and decided who was worth the while.

Anger, tears and sadness are only for those who have given up.

It had been confirmed. Things weren't good. The medical
team and my parents had decided between them that I would
be going down to theatre first thing in the morning. This
would be my first operation. They told me to try and sleep
because that's what my body needed and that tomorrow was
going to be another long day. I was right opposite the hospital
desk, on the ward. The nurses needed to keep an eye on me –
to keep me close to them. Just in case.

Mum and Dad were still conferring with the nursing staff about what was going to happen. As parents, they had a lot of unanswered questions. Would my eye be okay? Would I be able to see out of it? How much destruction had been done in my brain? Would I die?

The tiredness swept over my body once again, but it was going to be for the last time. This was a battle that I wasn't going to win. My body was so tired. I had been prodded and poked too long. Sleep was well and truly needed.

***

The hustle and bustle of the ward, of all the other sick children started early. I was awake, dazed, and unsure of where I was. Was this really happening? Surely if it was my subconscious, it would of ended by now or the course would have changed when my mind got bored. The pain had subsided. But I still wasn't allowed out of bed or to walk – at all.

I constantly had different people coming to check on me – taking my blood pressure and temperature, checking to see if I was feeling okay, and asking how my head was.

It was shortly after I woke up that the theatre team arrived to take me down for operation number one.

This one was to determine how bad it actually was and how much damage had really been caused. They began to wheel me down on the bed with my family following. The fear kicked in. Silent tears erupted and were pouring out. I was fighting back. I couldn't allow anyone to see this or to know that I was weak. I had never been so scared in my life.

What if I didn't make that journey back to the ward? What if this was the end? All of those unanswered questions were whizzing around my head.

Mum was stroking my hand, and reassuring me it was going to be okay. My dad was really upset. He was walking behind me. He didn't want me to see him crumbling. He was trying to stay strong for me, but I knew it was my job to be strong for them.

Dad offered me anything – anything I wanted – for being so brave. He said I could have whatever I wanted. I thought about it briefly, but there wasn't anything I wanted more than Tom – my puppy. So it was settled. Tom was mine.

We shortly arrived at theatre, after travelling back through the maze of the hospital. The medical team talked me through everything, as this was my first ever operation. They put some medicine into my cannula. It tasted horrid. Then they put a mask on my face with a funny blue light. The tingling started in my hand and then travelled up my arm in the back of my throat. I was drifting into somewhere far from this hell. Somewhere that numbed my body. And took all of the hell of this day with it. My eyelids went heavy. They wouldn't stay open. My words started being slurred. I was out, flat out until further notice.

I was in theatre whilst they repaired the damage that had been done for two hours. The surgical team patched everything up the best they could. During the operation they saw how severely damaged my right eye actually was. I had an irregular laceration to the sclera, which is the white bit of my eye. The tear went back eleven millimetres towards the optic nerve.

Your eye is made up of three layers; the middle pigmented layer of mine was prolapsing through the gap. I still had blood in my anterior chamber, which is the bit between your iris and your cornea. I had a large tear in my iris, and it was distorted around my eye. The muscles attached to the back of the eye were divided into two. The surgical team had to put them back together the best they could and insert the rectus muscle back into the eye. The rectus muscle is the muscle that allows you to turn your eye to look into the centre of your body.

***

My eyes opened, hazily. I was so tired, and all I wanted to do was to sleep. I was transported back up to the ward. I was pretty sleepy for a long while afterwards. I was bandaged up from the operation.

There was a lot more talking and conferring with my parents after this operation – about what had happened, where the pellet had travelled, and the damage it had caused. The surgical team explained what they had repaired, but people feared the worst for my eye and that it wasn't going to be able to be saved. Over the next few days, the outcome would be known. But they knew that, since the operation, I no longer had light awareness through the eye.

***

It had been three days since the accident, and I had visitors for the first time. My aunties and my grandparents were there. They were all very emotional. I think it was the not knowing. But it was good to see them. Grandma walked in and cried at the sight of me. I just sat on my bed and told her that I was okay. I was so happy to see everyone, and I knew that their visits would do Mum good. She and dad hadn't left my side.

On the days that followed the operation, I had get well soon cards and messages from people I wasn't sure even knew I existed. If this was how society was – that something big like this had to happen to your life for you to become noticed – then life itself was messed up. I'd never wish how I felt through this on anyone in a million years.

Here are some excerpts from my diary during that period:

DATE: 20.10.2003.
WEATHER: Dry and warm
WISH OF THE DAY: For my eye to get better
FAVOURITE FRIEND: My best mate
SPECIAL SECRET: I could lose my eye.
WHAT MAKES ME SAD: Being in hospital?
WHAT MAKES ME SMILE: Having my mum dad with me.
THOUGHTS OF LOVE: To go home to my family and puppy, Tom!

I am in Birmingham Children's Hospital with a poorly eye, as I was shot! I may or probably will lose my eye and have to have a false one. I am going to have a patch and some tinted glasses to wear to cover it. Mum and Dad have bought me a puppy called Tom. The puppy is thirteen weeks old and is a golden retriever.

***

DATE: 21.10.2003.
WEATHER: Dry and cold
WISH OF THE DAY: For the doctors to let me go home
FAVOURITE FRIEND: My mum
SPECIAL SECRET: I own a puppy.
WHAT MAKES ME SAD: I may not be able to go home.
WHAT MAKES ME SMILE: Tom!!!
THOUGHTS OF LOVE: For my eye

I went to the eye department today. They said that it was more than certain that I would be having an enucleation (the removal of my eye). I was upset. But I know it's for the best. I was able to go home today, but I have to go back early in the morning, so we decided to stay in Birmingham Children's Hospital one last time before the next operation.

***

On 22 October 2003, I had a visual function test and an ophthalmic ultrasound. The results showed severe disruption and completely absent electrophysiological function. That means there was no activity in my eye.

DATE: 22.10.2003
WEATHER: Dry and chilly
WISH OF THE DAY: For the scans to prove okay and that my eye's going to be okay
FAVOURITE FRIEND: Me
SPECIAL SECRET: I am scared.
WHAT MAKES ME SAD: The inside of my eye?

WHAT MAKES ME SMILE: The thought of it all being okay
THOUGHTS OF LOVE: For Tom

Today I went for an electrode test at Birmingham City Eye Hospital as I was discharged! The only bad bit is, if the test on my eye is negative, I will lose my eye on 24/10/2003. It has upset me, but I know it's for the best else. It would destroy my good eye, which I do not want to happen. So I think it will be best all round!

***

After the eye hospital appointment, I got to go home. Mum and Dad had bought me a new outfit to leave the hospital, as the clothes I'd been admitted in were covered in blood. I was able to go and get my puppy and spend some time with him. I remember seeing people for the first time. Everyone was so worried. Why? I was fine. Right? My brother cried. It must have been hard for him, I was dragging our parents away from him to be with me, and it was selfish. It hurt, but the truth was I'd never needed them as much as I did right now. Their strength and support was going to help me through the next challenging few weeks of my life, as I knew I wasn't out of the woods just yet.

It was great to see the people I loved, and it showed how much they cared and how many people actually had taken an interest. I had presents at home from the surrounding neighbours and people popping over to check if I was okay.

There wasn't much of the day left. It was late, and with all the medication I was on, I was quite sleepy. I was helped into bed, and I was out for the night.

Tomorrow, when it arrived, was going to be good. I knew it.

THE ENUCLEATION

So, come with me where dreams are born
And time is never planned.
Just think of happy things, and your heart will fly on wings.

I know everything happens for a reason,
but sometimes I wish I knew that.

I hope everyone that is reading this is having a really good day.
And if you are not,
Just know that, in every minute that passes, you
have an opportunity to change that...
I did!
Otherwise, you won't live your life to its full
potential, and you'll be left with regrets.
If I didn't change it, I would have been left with nothing.

The next morning seemed bright. I had slept well and woke up feeling normal, just like me. Maybe it was all a nightmare? Mum came in shortly after I woke to help me get out of bed, dressed, and down the stairs. I soon realised that the nightmare was the present, and I was going to be stuck in it for some time yet.

Grandma came round shortly after I got up. Today was the day I had to go and buy my puppy's collar and lead so that I could go and collect him. Even if it was for just a night and then I was back in, getting Tom was the distraction I needed.

We got into the car and went to the pet shop. I chose everything I needed for Tom – a puppy collar, a lead, a bowl, toys, food, and a name tag. I was so excited, but I was also completely exhausted. Just doing a small amount of stuff had tired me out.

When we got home, I was so excited to go and collect Tom. I went in the house to show Dad and Mark what we had purchased. They said that if I wanted him, I had to go and collect him alone. It was the first time I had been alone in a week. I left the house to cross the road, carrying the lead. I knocked on the door. I was let into the neighbour's house and was told Tom was in the garden. I went straight through to see him.

I remember seeing him for the first time and thinking, *Yes! He's mine.* I put his lead and collar on him and left through the side gate and went home.

He was lovely, so gentle and caring. It was like he knew that there was something wrong. He never left my feet. But he snuck around when he needed to as to not knock me or jump up and catch my eye.

DATE: 23.10.2003.

WEATHER: Dry and windy

WISH OF THE DAY: For everything to go okay with the enucleation tomorrow

FAVOURITE FRIEND: Tom

SPECIAL SECRET: After tomorrow, I will own a puppy and a false eye.
WHAT MAKES ME SAD: Being worried about the operation?
WHAT MAKES ME SMILE: Being around my family?
THOUGHTS OF LOVE: For me and for tomorrow to go okay

Today was great. I got my puppy. His name is Tom, and he is a thirteen-week-old golden retriever. He has a favourite toy that he plays with called a raggie. I love him so much. Tomorrow makes me sad, though, as I'll be having my eye removed.

Today was the day. Today was the day that I'd go from being a normal teen to somebody with a false eye. Nerves were bubbling up inside of me. I don't think *scared* is even the best word to describe the feelings I had. But I knew it was for the best. My eye has started to open, and my real eye did not look good. The black pupil was in the corner by my tear duct, and the iris was shattered like a piece of glass and scattered all over my eyeball.

DATE: 24.10.2003
WEATHER: Dry and windy
WISH OF THE DAY: For my eye swelling to go down
FAVOURITE FRIEND: Dad
SPECIAL SECRET: I am halfway to having my eye properly done
WHAT MAKES ME SAD: It itches and people's reaction
WHAT MAKES ME SMILE: White Maltesers and reassurance?
THOUGHTS OF LOVE: For nobody to laugh at me

Today I travelled to Birmingham Children's hospital again. We left the house at 5.00 a.m. When I got there, I had some people to speak to me. We painted boxes – a heart-shaped one, a black and white one, and an egg cup, and we looked at the false eyes.

I was able to be walked down to theatre this time, as I was mobile. It was about 2.30 p.m. I got changed into the hospital gown, put my slippers and dressing gown on, and started the walk that felt like forever, following the nurse to the theatre to meet the surgeon. I carried my doll under my arm. She wore her matching hospital band so she wouldn't get lost. I didn't care if people thought I was too old to be carrying a doll. I was thirteen, and I was petrified. My world had just been spun upside down. The carpet had been pulled from under my feet, and she was the only thing that would be the same in my life.

I had magic numbing cream on the back of my hands, which the nurses had applied in preparation for my cannula to be fitted at theatre. When I got to the room, there were lots of people there, all telling me who they were and what their jobs were. I felt someone grab my hand and take off the plaster. They wiped away the magic cream. It felt weird, like my hand was made of cotton wool. I didn't even feel them put the cannula in.

The next thing they asked me to do was count as high as I could. I knew they had put the anaesthetic into the cannula. My hand began to tingle, and the horrid taste arrived at the back of my throat. They put a mask over my face with a blue light for the second time.

One… Two… Three. Then nothing. I was out. I drifted away into a deep sleep. I was out for about three hours this time.

They had decided it was for the best. They had told us that there was a risk of severe sympathetic endophthalmitis, which is inflammation of the anterior and posterior chambers. The decision was also based on cosmetic appearance, which would be extremely poor with a disordered pupil, hyphaema (blood pooling in the front chamber of my eye), and a divergent squint where my eyes were never looking the same way.

***

When I woke, I was drowsy. My head was heavy on the one side. It was fuzzy. Mum and Dad were both there in resuscitation talking to me as I was coming back round. I remember people talking to me. They asked me questions about where I was and what day it was. All I wanted to do was sleep. They handed me a big green button, explaining that I was to press it when I was in pain, as it was connected to morphine, and it would help. After that, they transported me back up to the ward with my parents walking alongside the moving bed.

I have had my eye operation done now. It is sore and really itchy, but it is well padded up with a big bandage.

I couldn't wait for the morning to arrive. It had been a long day, and all I was wishing for was to be discharged so I could return home to my puppy, Tom!

MY NEW EYE

Believe in yourself! Have faith in your abilities!
Without a humble but reasonable confidence in your
own powers, you cannot be successful or happy.
Peace begins with me starting over and breaking free.
Peace starts with a smile.

After yet another night in hospital, I was woken every hour through the night for hourly observations. Carers routinely checked my eye and blood pressure and administered drugs for pain relief. It was finally breakfast time. Yum! Because I was a teenager, I was farther on down the ward, and by the time the breakfast tray reached me, the choice was soggy cornflakes and cold toast.

I was finally discharged, and by the time the nurses had done the paperwork and took my cannula out, it was mid-morning. We left the hospital and made our back to Leominster. I was so sick. The first time people saw me, they became upset. Why? Was I really that different since the accident? If so, I would be even more different now.

My auntie and uncle would be coming up tonight, Mum and Dad said. I hadn't seen a lot of family since the accident, and they would be driving down from Shrewsbury.

When we got back home, I went in the house and sat down. I was tired. No matter how little I'd done, nowadays I was always tired. Dad went and put Tom on his lead, as they were worried he would be too excited to see me, jump up, and knock my eye. But he wasn't. He crept in slowly, crawling like a baby. It was as if he sensed it. He was completely calm but chose never to leave my side. This puppy was amazing. It was like he knew what was going on and that he had to be gentle.

DATE: 25.10.2003
WEATHER: Windy
WISH OF THE DAY: For this to be over soon
FAVOURITE FRIEND: My auntie
SPECIAL SECRET: My false eye is dark brown/black
WHAT MAKES ME SAD: Seeing the lead pellets from the police
WHAT MAKES ME SMILE: Everyone
THOUGHTS OF LOVE: For everyone to stop worrying

I got discharged again today, this time for a week. Then I have to go back in for a week to have the lead pellet removed.

My false eye has been fitted. The only problem is, it's dark brown and stings a little.

I love my puppy, Tom, and I'd like everyone to stop worrying and crying!!!

I felt so confused at the moment. My head was swimming. I didn't know whether I should laugh or cry. How should I be feeling about my new eye? Were there written instructions on what to feel and which parts of your life to feel them at? If there was, I wished I'd been given a copy of the written handbook. All I knew was 'I am fine' works wonders and people believe it. Don't they?

DATE: 26.10.2003
WEATHER: Chilly
WISH OF THE DAY: To get better
FAVOURITE FRIEND: Mum and Dad
SPECIAL SECRET: Dad's buying me some glasses
WHAT MAKES ME SAD: They're to cover my false eye?
WHAT MAKES ME SMILE: Thumb wars
THOUGHTS OF LOVE: For Tom!

Today Mum, Dad, and myself went to take Tom for a walk. We let him off the lead for the first time. He was so good. He didn't run off. He just stayed and walked by my side!!

We went down to our friends the Parkers for tea. We took Tom with us. He was very well behaved. Tomorrow I am going back to hospital.

That night I slept silently once the pain had subsided, but the headaches had begun.

The next morning, I woke with a start. Another nightmare. Flashing images. And a loud *bang*.

Today when I woke, I had a hospital appointment at Hereford County Hospital to remove the bandages that were covering my new false eye. It was time for it to be revealed.

I got ready for the day ahead. Painkillers. Breakfast. Getting washed and dressed. Normal lifetime routine. We soon were all ready to leave. I felt good. Dad had said I could go and choose my glasses to wear to hide my eye.

We arrived at the hospital, and went through to the Eign Eye Suite. This place would now become a huge part of my life with all the regular check-ups that would be needed. We sat and waited for my name to be called. It felt like forever. I was waiting for my name to be called for the start of my life sentence.

Someone called my name and led me down to the treatment room at the end of the long corridor. In the room, there was a trolley with a lamp with some bits like sterile water and cleaning things and a couch. I lay down. They used the water to wet the plasters holding the bandage on to stop it from pulling too much. They slowly eased the corners of the plaster, lifting the bandage off completely.

Welcome to the world my new eye.

I looked in the mirror at the damage. My eye was black. Green. Yellow. Purple. It was swollen. It was hideous. Now we had to walk up town to the shop to choose my glasses.

Everyone stared. Well that's how it felt. They must have been curious. It was one thing I was going to have to get used too. People staring. Seeing a thirteen-year-old girl with a swollen and bruised eye and nose was probably not a normal thing to witness. Maybe I should cut them some slack?

DATE: 27.10.2003
WEATHER: Freezy
WISH OF THE DAY: For my eye not to look too bad
FAVOURITE FRIEND: My family
SPECIAL SECRET: I am scared!
WHAT MAKES ME SAD: My medicine?
WHAT MAKES ME SMILE: Seeing my friends
THOUGHTS OF LOVE: For my Dad!

Today we went to Hereford. I had my dressing taken off the poorly eye. Ouch!! It hurt.

Dad took me into town after to choose some glasses to hide my eye. They are really nice. I also bought some clothes and a game for the computer. The game is really good.

I love my family so much. They have stuck by me through everything, and I'm so touched that people really do care so much!!

***

DATE: 29.10.2003
WEATHER: Sunny and cold
WISH OF THE DAY: For my new eye to open fully
FAVOURITE FRIEND: Dad – because he puts a smile on my face

SPECIAL SECRET: I need my family so much and I love them.
WHAT MAKES ME SAD: Me – sometimes
WHAT MAKES ME SMILE: Me – sometimes
THOUGHTS OF LOVE: Me – sometimes

My favourite word today is *me*. Not a lot has happened today. I walked Tom, ate, and played on my new computer game.

The Parkers popped up today with their friend to say hi!

The police called by today to ask me some questions about my eye.

***

DATE: 30.10.2003
WEATHER: Wet
WISH OF THE DAY: For everyone
FAVOURITE FRIEND: Mum
SPECIAL SECRET: We're going shopping!
WHAT MAKES ME SAD: Rain
WHAT MAKES ME SMILE: Shopping
THOUGHTS OF LOVE: For my auntie and cousin!

Today, I was a little sick this morning. Again.

Mum, my auntie and cousin, and I went on a walk with Tom, and we let him off his lead.

We then went to Hereford, and I bought some clothes and accessories. Mum paid for it. I was so lucky. I love her so much.

When we got back from Hereford, we sat down as a family and watched *Spiderman*.

***

Date: 31.10.2003
Weather: Wet and cold
Wish of the Day: For Christmas to come quickly
Favourite Friend: Mum
Special Secret: My eye kept popping out, and it felt strange.
What Makes Me Sad: I am odd!
What Makes Me Smile: Seeing my friends
Thoughts of Love: For my eye – again!

Today is *Halloween*. A few family members came up. We had a few nibbles and a drink. We had a really good laugh.

Earlier today, I went to the hospital to speak to the police. It was so scary. But I know it was important. My eye started to slide out at the end of the videoed interview and started to hurt.

***

Date: 1.11.2003
Weather: Wet and cold
Wish of the Day: For no one to laugh at me

Favourite Friend: The chocolate box
Special Secret: I am feeling really low and scared of my eye.
What Makes Me Sad: My eye
What Makes Me Smile: Nothing at the moment
Thoughts of Love: For Mum and Dad to stop worrying

Today I could have cried. I was so low. My eye really made me stand out, and it always will. And my head hurts a lot.

Also I went down to town, and I felt people looking. We called into Martins Models and Craft in Leominster. It's a lovely shop, and the owners are lovely. The owners said that I could go and help her on a Saturday for a couple of hours and play with the toys.

That was good, but my eye is not. It is scary and ugly and odd, and it makes me feel so *down*!!

***

Date: 2.11.2003
Weather: Very wet
Wish of the Day: For school to go okay in the morning
Favourite Friend: Mum – because she says she loves me
Special Secret: My eye could pop out.
What Makes Me Sad: People worrying and crying.
What Makes Me Smile: People saying that they love me!
Thoughts of Love: For me going to school

Today the family came up for roast beef. It was lovely. I played in my bedroom.

Tomorrow I'll be returning to school just for the morning to say hi. It will be so nice to see my friends again.

I am starting to get bored at home. That's why I'm going to sew myself a bag.

That night I slept well, but I had a nervous feeling in my tummy. I wondered how people were going to react and be with me now. Would it be the same as before? Did they all know what had happened?

DAYS TO FOLLOW

7 steps to happiness

1) Think less, feel more.
2) Frown less, smile more.
3) Talk less, listen more.
4) Judge less, accept more.
5) Watch less, do more.
6) Complain less, appreciate more.
7) Fear less, love more.
Strength is a daily, a weekly, a monthly process,
gradually changing opinions, slowly eroding old
barriers, quietly building new structures.

Throughout this journey so far I had been schooled from my bedside, given homework to do while sitting in my bed and then eventually when I got home in between going back and forth to hospital. I was being picked up on a Friday to be taken to hospital school. It was Friday mornings. It was good and helped with me whether I was hurting or sick. But not today. I woke early, still having that unsettled feeling, which was horrible. I didn't know what the day was going to bring. I put my school uniform on and went down to have breakfast.

I got ready as I always did and did my hair. I knew I would only be in school for the morning, just to wean me back into it and to see how I got along. Mum was going to be taking me today. She had already spoken to the teachers to let them know all the details of how I was, what to do in case anything should happen, and what my needs were.

We left the house and parked at Mum's work. My best mate and I, along with Mum, walked around from there. School was exactly the same as it normally was. People were bustling around and walking in their friendship groups to get to tutorial and to where there meant to be.

We got to the school entrance. We walked through the doors and up the entrance stairs together. We walked round the corner and down the corridor. We were heading for the top playground and the science, English, and maths block. We went through the double doors and up the stairs to arrive on the playground.

It was the normal hustle and bustle of the playground – excited people chatting away to their friends and laughing. Then I was spotted. And silence. The whole playground stopped, turned, and stared. There was silence. You could hear a pin drop. I had people who had never spoken nicely to me before or even acknowledged me running over to me in tears to throw their arms around me and tell me how much I'd been missed.

The teachers soon arrived. They hurried everyone into their lines and straight into tutor. I was the talk of the school.

I knew then that life had changed in more than one way and one aspect.

I only had two lessons to do today, as I was going to be going home. But it was the same in each class – questions and people looking.

Date: 3.11.2003
Weather: Chilly
Wish of the Day: For mum to stop worrying
Favourite Friend: My school friends
Special Secret: I went to school this morning.
What Makes Me Sad: When people stare
What Makes Me Smile: Saying, 'Have you never seen eyes before?'
Thoughts of Love: For my family

Today I went to school for the morning. It was great. It was so nice to see everyone. My eye felt really funny today though, and by the end of the day, my eyebrow was aching, and I had a headache coming.

Tomorrow I'm going to school again, and I'll be starting to make my bag. I have to go to sleep early, as I have to be up early to feed, water, hug, walk, and play with Tom!

***

Date: 4.11.2003
Weather: Dry and chilly
Wish of the Day: For everything to go okay at Birmingham Children's Hospital tomorrow at my outpatient appointment
Favourite Friend: My best friend, as she makes me laugh

SPECIAL SECRET: I'm worried about tomorrow!
WHAT MAKES ME SAD: Being away from Tom
WHAT MAKES ME SMILE: Being with Tom
THOUGHTS OF LOVE: For my friends and teachers

Today I went to school, and I was in art when my eye fell out. The school rang Mum straight away, and I had to get her to come and put it back in, as I'm not used to doing it yet.

Tomorrow I have to go back to Birmingham Children's for an outpatient appointment to have tests done and to talk to the doctors about the stray pellet and to see if it has to be removed.

***

DATE: 5.11.2003
WEATHER: Dry and mild
WISH OF THE DAY: For whatever the doctors say
FAVOURITE FRIEND: Dad
SPECIAL SECRET: Mr Reed hurt my nose with the microscope.
WHAT MAKES ME SAD: I may lose my sense of smell.
WHAT MAKES ME SMILE: It actually may all be over.
THOUGHTS OF LOVE: For me

Today I went back to Birmingham Children's Hospital to talk to the doctors. Mr Reed really hurt my nose when he had to put a microscope up it to see if he could see anything. He told me that, if I choose to have the lead pellet removed, I may lose my sense of smell. But if I choose to leave it where it is, then it will most probably become infected.

***

DATE: 7.11.2003
WEATHER: Cold
WISH OF THE DAY: For my mates
FAVOURITE FRIEND: All of my mates
SPECIAL SECRET: I feel ill, all shivery.
WHAT MAKES ME SAD: Thinking sad thoughts
WHAT MAKES ME SMILE: My mates coming over.
THOUGHTS OF LOVE: For my bestest mate

Today my school friends came over for tea. My best mate came up to play, and a childhood friend called by. I was at school with him from when we started. We were inseparable, always going to each other houses and playing together. It was nice of him and his mum to call in to see if I was okay.

The bestie ended up staying the night tonight. We played on my brand-new computer game most of the night. It is really, really good.

***

DATE: 8.11.2003
WEATHER: Chilly

Wɪsʜ ᴏꜰ ᴛʜᴇ Dᴀʏ: For my grandma, who I love so much –
she means the world to me
Fᴀᴠᴏᴜʀɪᴛᴇ Fʀɪᴇɴᴅ: Everyone
Sᴘᴇᴄɪᴀʟ Sᴇᴄʀᴇᴛ: I am frozen.
Wʜᴀᴛ Mᴀᴋᴇs Mᴇ Sᴀᴅ: Being cold
Wʜᴀᴛ Mᴀᴋᴇs Mᴇ Sᴍɪʟᴇ: Being happy
Tʜᴏᴜɢʜᴛs ᴏꜰ Lᴏᴠᴇ: For our family friend

Today I did hardly anything. I watched some television
and played on the computer.

Tonight we had Chinese with our friends. It was lovely.
We all went outside and watched the eclipse of the moon.
It turned red and then disappeared.

***

Dᴀᴛᴇ: 9.11.2003
Wᴇᴀᴛʜᴇʀ: Freezy
Wɪsʜ ᴏꜰ ᴛʜᴇ Dᴀʏ: For Christmas and New Year to
come soon
Fᴀᴠᴏᴜʀɪᴛᴇ Fʀɪᴇɴᴅ: The bestie
Sᴘᴇᴄɪᴀʟ Sᴇᴄʀᴇᴛ: I am going to ask for a big party for
New Year.
Wʜᴀᴛ Mᴀᴋᴇs Mᴇ Sᴀᴅ: That Christmas is 46 days away –
it's ages to wait.
Wʜᴀᴛ Mᴀᴋᴇs Mᴇ Sᴍɪʟᴇ: The thought of next year being
a good one?
Tʜᴏᴜɢʜᴛs ᴏꜰ Lᴏᴠᴇ: For 2004!

Today I went for a walk with Tom twice.

I played on my amazing computer game.

I had two of my friends from school call around with get-well cards to see if I'm okay.

I had my best friend over so that we could hang out.

I love my family. Tomorrow I am returning to school full-time.

∗∗∗

Date: 10.11.2003
Weather: Dry and cold
Wish of the Day: For my mum
Favourite Friend: My bestie
Special Secret: I am going shopping for Christmas.
What Makes Me Sad: My tummy
What Makes Me Smile: Shopping
Thoughts of Love: For my bestest friend ever

Today it was her birthday. She was twelve years old. We have decided to go Christmas shopping to Cheltenham. It is going to be so much fun.

∗∗∗

Date: 11.11.2003
Weather: Damp and chilly

WISH OF THE DAY: For Christmas
FAVOURITE FRIEND: Grandma
SPECIAL SECRET: I love her so much.
WHAT MAKES ME SAD: Going to school
WHAT MAKES ME SMILE: Seeing my mates
THOUGHTS OF LOVE: For the bestie and her Nanna

Today I went to school for a full day. After school, I played on the computer and with Tom. My best mate popped up, and we hung out most of the night.

On Friday I am going to my other friend's for tea. Then on Saturday, I am off to Cheltenham Christmas shopping.

***

DATE: 12.11.2003
WEATHER: Wet and cold
WISH OF THE DAY: For Christmas to come soon.
FAVOURITE FRIEND: Mum
SPECIAL SECRET: I saw a shooting star
WHAT MAKES ME SAD: My silly eye
WHAT MAKES ME SMILE: Reassurance
THOUGHTS OF LOVE: For my school

I went to school today. We did, English, PSE, RE, and other things. I had an interview today to be a librarian. Fingers crossed that I get it.

When I got home from school, my grandma was here. I said that I loved her a lot. She said she loved me too but wished there was more she could do.

****

DATE: 13.11.2003
WEATHER: Chilly
WISH OF THE DAY: For my grandma
FAVOURITE FRIEND: My dad
SPECIAL SECRET: I didn't go to school today
WHAT MAKES ME SAD: My silly eye
WHAT MAKES ME SMILE: Love
THOUGHTS OF LOVE: For my family

Today I didn't go to school. I was so annoyed with my silly eye. I wish everything will be normal soon! I can then get on with what has been done, as I am stuck like this for the rest of my life. Now is the time to start anew!

RECOGNITION

All we are saying is give peace a chance.
Peace is a journey of a thousand miles

A lot of people don't want to make their own decisions.
They're too scared.
It's much easier to be told what to do.
And it must be taken one step at a time.

"Wake up, Claire! Get ready for school, put those clean trousers and shirt on, and put your hair up!"

Mum never told me what to wear for school or how to do my hair, but today she was taking an interest. So I just went with it. I put my on tight grey flare school trousers. They fitted well. After donning a clean shirt, I combed my hair and tied it up in a ponytail. I put my glasses on and went downstairs. Mum was already sitting on the sofa getting her work stuff ready, so I went into the kitchen to grab my lunch.

The bestie met us outside at 8.20, and we all got into the car. We laughed and chatted. Mum had work, so Dad would be picking us up after school from the normal place.

As soon as we pulled into the car park at the place Mum worked, the bestie and I got out the car and grabbed our stuff.

Mum took her work bag and started into work. Charlotte and I shouted, 'See ya later,' and started the walk round to school. We were talking between us and planning stuff to do later. We walked down the side of the school and then round towards the front doors, joining in with the crowd on the way down.

We got through the crowd and were redirected into the big hall through the big doors. There was a big assembly for all up to year ten. Great. The chairs were already put out. Year sevens were by the stage, and the years following behind them sat in tutorial groups. My tutor was near the back. We were all hurried in and sat in rows. I was near the aisle. At least I could see the front. I think they probably sat me there because of my eye and that they felt sorry for me.

The hall started filling up. I was looking around for my friends, as we were in different tutors, trying to find them in the crowd. Everyone was talking and shouting at each other. According to the talk, it was a special assembly. Someone next to me said, "Claire, you're getting an award."

Noooo! I thought.

My seatmate went on to say that it had been announced on the radio this morning. Why hadn't I heard it? Well, we hadn't listened to the radio this morning.

"No. You must have gotten it wrong," I told him.

There were a few people saying it now. I just sat there, thinking they were just saying it — till someone tapped me on the shoulder. "Isn't that your parents sitting at the back of the hall?"

I turned around. Sure enough, my mum and dad were at the back of the hall. I felt sick. Nervous. Scared.

The head teacher and the deputies walked down the aisle from the back of the hall, and we all stood in silence. People who I didn't recognise were sitting on the stage.

"Good morning, everyone" said the head teacher.

"Good morning," the lot of us chanted back.

"Please be seated," she said. "Today we are joined for a very special occasion. We have a massive honour. There is a pupil in our school who has shown bravery and courage against all odds."

My insides were bubbling up inside I knew she was talking about me. I was the only person in the school to have gone through anything like I had.

"We have a great honour of being joined this morning by the local MP. We nominated this student for the Princess Diana Memorial Award, and she has received it."

The entire room was silent as the teachers, in procession, stood to say their bits. One at a time, they talked about bravery and courage and what those things meant to them and gave out words of wisdom to the entire assemblage.

Then the deputy head stood to announce that it gave him immense pleasure to be able to announce that they were presenting Claire Davies with the Princess Diana Memorial Award, and could she make her way up to the stage.

Everyone was going mad, clapping and cheering. Turning bright red, I stood and started walking up through the aisle.

When I got to the stage, there were steps! Gulp! I hated stairs, and everything still being new, I still was struggling a bit. So the deputy head walked down the stairs and gave me his arm to help guide me up the stairs. I was so grateful. The MP presented me with the award, speaking about how much of an honour it was. He shook my hand before handing me a framed certificate and a little box with a silver lapel pin badge in it.

I said thank you, beaming from ear to ear, proud of how much I had achieved. I'd never been noticed before, and now I was having assemblies held – for me.

I got helped back down the stage stairs and made my way to my seat as everyone stood and applauded. I could see Mum and Dad at the back. They looked so proud and were smiling and applauding me.

I sat back down, and everyone was asking me to see the award and to have a look at what I had just gotten. The assembly was brought to a close, and everyone filed out to go to his or her lessons – everyone except me. I made my way to the back of the hall. Everyone hugged me and shook my hand and congratulated me.

The newspapers were there, their photographers ready to take pictures. Once the crowd of pupils had gone, we were escorted outside to the seating area. I posed for photographs with the teachers and with the head and with the MP for Leominster. And I had to give the reporters my story and tell them that I hadn't known anything about any of it – the nomination, the assembly, the award. Well I didn't – not until I sat down just before the assembly was about to begin.

Once all the photos had been taken, I had to go and join my class in geography. As I walked up the block and then up two flights of stairs, I knew that this wasn't going to be the last of it.

Today was going to be good – good but full of questions, congratulations, and endless curiosity evoking endless versions of, 'Can I see it?'

THE START OF USING BAD TO PRODUCE GOOD

If you were made to wear thorns,
Twist them and shape them
Into something beautiful.

There is good in every bad. Isn't there? There is a way to make something negative into something positive. There must be a way to use this negative life experience to help others in the form of something good. No matter what I went through and what was sent my way, as long as others were helped and were smiling at the end of it, then it was all worth it. I was determined to use my negative experiences to become positive. Now being the proud owner of the Princess Diana Memorial Award, I was left wondering how far I could take it – how much of the 'One-Eyed Child' sob-story perks I could get and how I could use them to help others. Because that would be good – using a bad experience to help others have a positive one.

DATE: 18.11.2003
WEATHER: Dry and windy
WISH OF THE DAY: For tomorrow to go well

Favourite Friend: Tom
Special Secret: Tomorrow, I have to make 500 eyepatches in two hours.
What Makes Me Sad: I may not achieve it.
What Makes Me Smile: Being positive
Thoughts of Love: For my mum

Today I went to school as normal. But tomorrow, I am going to school to make 500 eyepatches in two hours. That equals three a minute. We will then be selling them in the school to every student and teacher to benefit children in need. Everyone then for the day or a few hours will see just how it is to be me, even if it is just temporary.

So far I have raised just over £50. Wow!!

***

Date: 19.11.2003
Weather: Chilly
Wish of the Day: For the 500 eyepatches
Favourite Friend: Myself
Special Secret: I'm having my hair cut and coloured tomorrow.
What Makes Me Sad: Going to the solicitors
What Makes Me Smile: Having my hair done
Thoughts of Love: For fizz

I did it!!!!! I made all 500 eyepatches in two hours. So now for children in need, I will sell them to the school :)

Tomorrow I have to go to the solicitors :(

And I'm having my hair done. I get it cut and coloured all over, and I can't wait :)

***

Date: 20.11.2003
Weather: Drizzly
Wish of the Day: For my hair
Favourite Friend: My mum
Special Secret: I get my hair cut and coloured today.
What Makes Me Sad: Having to go to the solicitors
What Makes Me Smile: Having my hair done
Thoughts of Love: For my dad

Today I had my hair done. I had it coloured all over. I have a darker brown all over, and then I had bright intense red streak running through it. It looks lovely, I'm so pleased with it, and I had a sweeping fringe cut into it to hide my stupid eye a bit.

We went to Hereford after and had a KFC, and then we went to the solicitors about my eye.

That afternoon was nice. We sat in the art room and made the 500 eyepatches during the last two hours of school. We completed the project. We were going to sell the patches to everyone at the school, giving everyone the chance to be like me for the day.

In the evening, we went to Hereford. The solicitors' office was quiet. The waiting room was upstairs, and it had big green leather sofas in a 'C' shape. It smelled funny. It was scary quiet, with rooms coming off the open landing. We sat there and waited for a couple of minutes with our Christmas shopping and other stuff.

This jolly happy smiling man started walking down the corridor to the open landing where we sat.

'Mr Davies,' he said, putting his hand out. 'It's nice to meet you.'

He shook Mum's hand the same, and Mum greeted him.

Then he shook my hand. He had a tight grip, but his hand was soft.

We followed him back down the corridor he had just walked up and into a small office. He had a massive desk in there, and a big chair behind it, along with a few chairs set out in front of it. We each took a seat and faced him.

He introduced himself. He was nice. He spoke to me and asked what I'd been buying. I was carrying a big box, which was my Christmas present. It was a new mobile phone, but it came with a stereo, which made the box massive. He laughed and said that, in that box, it looked like one of the mobiles that was massive and from the Stone Ages. The conversation made me feel comfortable and that being in that environment was okay.

He then started asking questions – lots of questions. It made me feel uncomfortable, and all eyes were on me. I told him what had happened. I explained where I was and what my friend and I were doing. He took lots of notes, writing it all down. After an hour with him asking questions and getting information, questions being fired back and forward between all three of us – Mum, Dad, and myself, he thanked me. After shaking all of our hands again, he walked us down the stairs and saw us out.

I could tell that this was going to be a long-haul thing, which was going to be dragged out. I'd have to constantly relive the experience and go over and over it. I knew that it would be something that would never be forgotten, and even if I wanted to, I didn't think I ever would.

This wasn't going to be the last meeting. It was the first of my lifetime.

AWARDS

If you are brave enough to just let go,
stand up, and face your demons,
Then and only then will you be faced with a new world.

DATE: 21.11.2003
WEATHER: Wet
WISH OF THE DAY: For me
FAVOURITE FRIEND: School friends
SPECIAL SECRET: I could have been on TV.
WHAT MAKES ME SAD: Being treated like I am silly
WHAT MAKES ME SMILE: Being famous
THOUGHTS OF LOVE: For me

Today was children in need.

I have raised over £400 so far by making and selling eyepatches.

I was on the radio and in two newspapers.

Over the next few weeks, I spent my time thinking about how I was able to use my story for the greater good – to make people aware that these things happen daily and to actually get justice. In my best handwriting, I wrote to the queen and to *Blue Peter*.

They both wrote back. The queen wrote a lovely letter, telling me that I was a brave young lady and saying how courageous I was. She congratulated me on the Princess Diana Memorial Award.

Blue Peter sent me the Gold Blue Peter Badge – the show's highest award, for bravery and courage. I was honoured. I was so proud that my story was actually touching people's hearts and that I was the recipient of these awards.

I was nominated for the West Mercia Police Good Citizen Award, which I went to receive in the town hall. They spoke to me about my story in front of the papers and cameras and went on to award me with a certificate and pin badge.

DATE: 22.11.2003
WEATHER: Dry
WISH OF THE DAY: For Mum and Dad
FAVOURITE FRIEND: Me
SPECIAL SECRET: It is Mum and Dad's wedding anniversary. They were meant to be having a Chinese dinner in Hong Kong. But because of my accident, they stayed with me.
WHAT MAKES ME SAD: My eye hurting
WHAT MAKES ME SMILE Having Chinese
THOUGHTS OF LOVE: For Grandma

Mum and Dad have been married for seventeen years.

We had Chinese for tea. :)

***

DATE: 23.11.2003
WEATHER: Wet
WISH OF THE DAY: For my auntie
FAVOURITE FRIEND: Mark, my brother
SPECIAL SECRET: We are going to Granny's for tea.
WHAT MAKES ME SAD: My eye hurting
WHAT MAKES ME SMILE: Hama beads
THOUGHTS OF LOVE: For Granddad

Today is Sunday.

I feel bad.

My eye hurts.

My head hurts.

***

DATE: 24.11.2003
WEATHER: Cold
WISH OF THE DAY: To get well
FAVOURITE FRIEND: Dad
SPECIAL SECRET: I did not go to school.
WHAT MAKES ME SAD: Having this infection
WHAT MAKES ME SMILE: Being with Dad
THOUGHTS OF LOVE: For Christmas

Today I didn't do much. I didn't go to school, as they think that I have an infection around the lead pellet and in my eye.

The newspapers came over today to take my photo.

***

DATE: 25.11.2003
WEATHER: Wet
WISH OF THE DAY: For me
FAVOURITE FRIEND: My best friend
SPECIAL SECRET: Bingo is on tonight.
WHAT MAKES ME SAD: Being infected
WHAT MAKES ME SMILE: Being with Dad
THOUGHTS OF LOVE: For school tomorrow

Today I made scones. I watched TV. We went down to Grannies. I played with Tom...and lots more.

Tonight I went to BINGO. It was really fun.

***

DATE: 26.11.2003
WEATHER: Wet and hail
WISH OF THE DAY: For Christmas
FAVOURITE FRIEND: My best friend
SPECIAL SECRET: Christmas is in twenty-nine days.
WHAT MAKES ME SAD: Waiting for it
WHAT MAKES ME SMILE: Christmas is nearly here.

Thoughts of Love: For Santa

It is *Christmas* in twenty-nine days.

Today I went back to school. It was boring.

I went home, I had my tea, and then I went to watch badminton.

I was in *The Journal* newspaper tonight.

I also received the community award and the bravery award that was created especially for me at the presentation evening at school.

Date: 27.11.2003
Weather: Cold
Wish of the Day: For my BCG
Favourite Friend: My best friend
Special Secret: She hurt herself.
What Makes Me Sad: Needles.
What Makes Me Smile: Christmas will soon be here.
Thoughts of Love: For me

Tomorrow I have my BCG, but enough about needles.

Today I was on TV.

We had my school presentation evening tonight. I was awarded a surprise bravery award. Everybody in the hall stood and clapped. I received a certificate and a £20 book token.

***

Date: 28.11.2003
Weather: Miserable
Wish of the Day: For my arm and for the bestie
Favourite Friend: My best friend
Special Secret: I had my BCG #1
What Makes Me Sad: The bestie's leg
What Makes Me Smile: Christmas is soon.
Thoughts of Love: For my school friends

Today I had my BCG #1.

I had a headache all day today. My best friend went to hospital today with a bad leg.

I really am happy. We're having a sleepover tonight, and we are going to go shopping tomorrow.

LIFE GOES ON

Do not pray for an easy life.
Pray for the strength to endure a difficult one.

DATE: 29.11.2003
WEATHER: Chilly
WISH OF THE DAY: For me and my bestest friend ever
FAVOURITE FRIEND: My bestie
SPECIAL SECRET: I went to the cinema, and I have a surprise for Mum.
WHAT MAKES ME SAD: My eye
WHAT MAKES ME SMILE: Me and my bestie – she just understands me
THOUGHTS OF LOVE: For mum

Christmas is nearly here! Yay!! And I'm counting down.

Tomorrow I have a surprise for Mum, and I cannot wait.

Mark has karate tomorrow, so my best mate and I will probably go too. I am so scared about Monday though. I am going to Birmingham Children's Hospital for a talk.

***

DATE: 30.11.2003
WEATHER: Wet
WISH OF THE DAY: For me because today I'm Moaning Myrtle
FAVOURITE FRIEND: Tom
SPECIAL SECRET: I am going to Birmingham Children's Hospital tomorrow
WHAT MAKES ME SAD: Seeing *more* doctors
WHAT MAKES ME SMILE: Making things okay
THOUGHTS OF LOVE: For tomorrow

It is 1 December tomorrow, meaning there will be twenty-four days :) yay!

Today I went to watch Mark at karate. Then I made some coffee cakes.

I played with Tom, my cousins, and my best friend.

***

DATE: 1.12.2003
WEATHER: Chilly
WISH OF THE DAY: For the next twenty-four days to go fast
FAVOURITE FRIEND: Bestie and my brother
SPECIAL SECRET: The doctors said I will have to have the lead pellet taken out.
WHAT MAKES ME SAD: Having operations

WHAT MAKES ME SMILE: Knowing no more headaches
THOUGHTS OF LOVE: For Mum and Dad

The doctors today said that I would have to have the lead pellet removed. Soon.

I was also sick today, outside next in Birmingham. I was so embarrassed.

***

DATE: 2.12.2003
WEATHER: Chilly
WISH OF THE DAY: For Christmas
FAVOURITE FRIEND: Dad
SPECIAL SECRET: I'm going shopping with my cousin.
WHAT MAKES ME SAD: My headaches
WHAT MAKES ME SMILE: Being loved
THOUGHTS OF LOVE: For my cousin on Friday

Twenty-three days left!!!

Today I came home early from school, as I was sick.

My cousin, Grannie, Granddad, and Auntie came up tonight, and tomorrow I am going out with them.

I cannot wait to shop!

***

DATE: 3.12.2003
WEATHER: Cold
WISH OF THE DAY: For cousin's operation on Friday
FAVOURITE FRIEND: My cousin
SPECIAL SECRET: She bought loads today.
WHAT MAKES ME SAD: My headaches
WHAT MAKES ME SMILE: Shopping
THOUGHTS OF LOVE: For my cousin

Twenty-two days left!!!

Today I was off school again, but today my cousin was down, so we went to Hereford shopping.

We had lunch and made cakes together. She is sleeping over tonight, and we are having a laugh. It's great fun.

***

DATE: 4.12.2003
WEATHER: Cold
WISH OF THE DAY: For mum
FAVOURITE FRIEND: My school friend
SPECIAL SECRET: I went to school.
WHAT MAKES ME SAD: I'm having my *big* BCG tomorrow.
WHAT MAKES ME SMILE: Seeing my family
THOUGHTS OF LOVE: For my cousin

Twenty-one days to go!!

Today I was asked to be a bridesmaid. So that means now I have to grow my hair and my nails.

Today I went to school. But I'm really scared, as tomorrow I have to have my *big* BCG.

***

DATE : 5.12.2003
WEATHER: Dry and chilly
WISH OF THE DAY: For Thursday
FAVOURITE FRIEND: Mum
SPECIAL SECRET: I had my *big* BCG TB jab.
WHAT MAKES ME SAD: It hurt.
WHAT MAKES ME SMILE: The pellet is coming out soon.
THOUGHTS OF LOVE: For my new eye

Twenty days left to go!!!

Today I had my last BCG jab. My arm now really aches.

Birmingham Children's Hospital rang today to see if I could have the lead pellet removed on Thursday.

Tomorrow I start my new little Saturday job. I'm nervous.

***

DATE: 6.12.2003
WEATHER: Cold
WISH OF THE DAY: For Thursday

Favourite Friend: Mum
Special Secret: I keep crying.
What Makes Me Sad: Crying
What Makes Me Smile: Working
Thoughts of Love: For the people at the shop

Nineteen days left!!!

Today I went to work. It got me out of the house for a couple of hours. It was brilliant. I helped out from noon to 4.00 p.m. It made me feel super.

I got in the end a £15 doll outfit for my Annabel, a set of bins for her, and loads of Hama beads.

When I got home, I started to worry about Thursday again. I spent the night in tears.

***

Date: 7.12.2003
Weather: Dry and cold
Wish of the Day: For my Grandma
Favourite Friend: I am going to shopping today and Wednesday.
Special Secret: Shopping
What Makes Me Sad: Going to hospital on Thursday
What Makes Me Smile:: Shopping
Thoughts of Love: For my Mum

Eighteen days left!!! Christmas is coming around fast. There are only eighteen days left, but first comes my operation.

I am so scared. It could all go horribly wrong. What if it does?

On Wednesday I'm going to Hereford to get the last few bits before I go into hospital.

***

Date: 8.12.2003
Weather: Cold
Wish of the Day: For Thursday and for Christmas
Favourite Friend: My school friends
Special Secret: I am scared about Thursday.
What Makes Me Sad: Being scared
What Makes Me Smile: That Christmas is coming soon
Thoughts of Love: For Tom and my family

Seventeen days to go!!!!

Tomorrow is my last day at school till the New Year, because I'm going to Hereford Wednesday for the last few bits ready for hospital on Thursday.

Hopefully I'll be able to get a new CD. It is now 56. It looks really good.

***

DATE: 9.12.2003
WEATHER: Cold
WISH OF THE DAY: For my last day at school
FAVOURITE FRIEND: My mates
SPECIAL SECRET: It's my last day at school.
WHAT MAKES ME SAD: Leaving everyone till New Year
WHAT MAKES ME SMILE: Sleeping at my grandma's
THOUGHTS OF LOVE: For my best friend

Sixteen days to go!!!

Today was my last day at school till after New Year.

I am really, really scared about Thursday.

I'm keeping over at Grandma's tonight.

I received a letter from one of the teachers.

***

DATE: 10.12.2003
WEATHER: Foggy
WISH OF THE DAY: For tomorrow
FAVOURITE FRIEND: The bestie
SPECIAL SECRET: I am going to hospital tomorrow.
WHAT MAKES ME SAD: Hospitals
WHAT MAKES ME SMILE: I will be pellet less.
THOUGHTS OF LOVE: For my best friend

Fifteen days left to go!!! Today I went to Hereford with my grandma. We went to get the last few bits I needed to take with me to hospital. I got socks, etc. I'm scared about tomorrow, but it has to be done.

THE REMOVAL OF THE LEAD PELLET

Dancing past the dark

DATE: 11.12.2003
WEATHER: Chilly
WISH OF THE DAY: For the operation
FAVOURITE FRIEND: Mum and Dad
SPECIAL SECRET: I am having the pellet removed from my brain.
WHAT MAKES ME SAD: Having it done?
WHAT MAKES ME SMILE: It being over with.
THOUGHTS OF LOVE: For me

Fourteen days left to go!!!

Today is the day.

I am so, so scared about this operation, but I know it has to be done, and I know that it is for the best.

It will mean no more infections.

The day had arrived. Gulp. Mum woke us crazy early – at 5 a.m. I had to get everything ready to go. I went downstairs and saw Tom, let him out into the garden, and spent a bit of time with him. I was allowed a small glass of water, but that was it because of the anaesthetic.

We arrived at the hospital. I clutched my doll. Mum and Dad walked with me carrying the bags as we made our way to Ward 5.

There had been lots of discussion about this operation, and the neurosurgeon whose care I had been under at the hospital had decided it would be best if someone else performed the surgery. It was a rare case, and none of the surgeons at the hospital had had a case where a child had a lead pellet lodged in her brain that needed removing. The neurosurgeon had said that, if he were to do it, he would have to shave my hair off – all of it – and then cut me ear to ear. He would have to break my skull and remove the top of it. He would then lift my brain out and remove the pellet. It was major surgery. It was serious, and he didn't want to put me through it. He would rather a member of the ENT surgical team dealt with it. The ENT specialist had never done an operation like this on a child. So they called the ENT specialist in from the Queen Elizabeth Birmingham Hospital. Because Queen Elizabeth was an adult hospital, the facility wouldn't care for a child there. So the specialist had to be called into Birmingham children's to perform the surgery.

We arrived at the ward, and I was admitted. I got tagged and shown to my bed. As I settled in, they came round to explain the operation to me and to put magic cream on the back of my hands once more.

The time came, and I was led down to theatre. I learned that I would be under for three to four hours. Mum and Dad followed me and the nurse. I wore my dressing gown and slippers and carried my baby doll. I lay on the bed, and someone from the surgical team took off the plasters, wiped the magic cream off, and inserted the cannula. Then the anaesthetist put the anaesthetic in. It was the same routine. The mask with the blue light went over my mouth and nose. I was told to count.

One... Two... Three ... And I was out.

During the operation, the surgical team performed septoplasty for access. That's where they straightened the middle partition in my nose between the two naval cavities. They then removed the uncinectomy and bulla. This is the first step in this type of surgery. They perforated the lamellar. The superior turbinate got excised, and the sphenoid opened. The back end of my septum was removed with a biting tool. The pellet was found within new bone formation. The bone was excised to get the pellet out. Basically it was a *big* operation with lots of complicated words.

Mum and Dad were escorted back up to the ward, where they were to sit and wait. They sat in my bay opposite the nurse's station for six hours before they finally got the phone call to say that I was in recovery.

They started to leave the ward and walk down to be with me. Meanwhile, I had woken up. The nurse ran after them. There had been a complication. I had had a bleed. She explained that it wasn't until I'd started to come around that they would know if I had, and I had. They had to put me back under and rush me back into theatre to stop the bleeding.

One and a half hours later, Mum and Dad were given the okay to go down to recovery, where I was. When they walked into see me, they faced a scene that looked like something from *The Texas Chainsaw Massacre.* The white sheet I was laying on and the one that was covering me were drenched in blood. I was covered from head to toe. It turned out I had had two brisk bleeds from my left nostril and had lost 250 millilitres in total. I had a flame-shaped haemorrhage on the right frontal part of my brain and some mass effect.

The next few days were going to be critical. We all knew that.

For the rest of the evening, I slept. I had a heavy head. And I hurt – a lot.

The next morning came, and I still hadn't woken up properly. My head felt heavy. Really heavy. Too heavy to hold up. I couldn't eat. And every time I moved my head, I was violently sick.

DATE: 12.12.2003
WEATHER: Looks windy
WISH OF THE DAY: For Me
FAVOURITE FRIEND: Everyone
SPECIAL SECRET: I am so tired.
WHAT MAKES ME SAD: Not waking up
WHAT MAKES ME SMILE: Mum
THOUGHTS OF LOVE: Dad and Mum

Thirteen days to go!!!

There is one word for me today and that is *sleepy*.

I still haven't woken up properly, the nurse said. Oh well.

Everyone was so worried about me during that period. My carers and parents were worried that I wasn't waking up from the anaesthesia. I could see their concern, and they kept encouraging me to stay awake. But I couldn't keep my eyes open.

DATE: 13.12.2003
WEATHER: Don't know
WISH OF THE DAY: For me
FAVOURITE FRIEND: My best mate
SPECIAL SECRET: She is coming to visit me.
WHAT MAKES ME SAD: I can't keep awake.
WHAT MAKES ME SMILE: People being here even if I am asleep
THOUGHTS OF LOVE: For my family, friends, and Tom

Twelve days to go now!!!

Today, yet again, I slept and slept.

Except for the ten minutes when my best friend was visiting. But I needed some sticks to hold my eyes open, and Mum kept waking me up.

***

DATE: 14.12.2003
WEATHER: Looks cold
WISH OF THE DAY: For the test
FAVOURITE FRIEND: Dad
SPECIAL SECRET: I have had a frontal lobe brain haemorrhage, and I could be epileptic.
WHAT MAKES ME SAD: This right now
WHAT MAKES ME SMILE: Getting out of here
THOUGHTS OF LOVE: To get out of here

Eleven days to go!!!

Today I had lots of tests and CT scans. This is because I am so sleepy. The tests have shown that I have had a brain haemorrhage.

The tests had revealed a new frontal lobe haemorrhage with surrounding oedema – fluid retention in the body that causes swelling.

DATE: 15.12.2003
WEATHER: Don't know
WISH OF THE DAY: For my headaches
FAVOURITE FRIEND: Dad and Mum
SPECIAL SECRET: I was still so sleepy.
WHAT MAKES ME SAD: Feeling this poorly
WHAT MAKES ME SMILE: Being awake
THOUGHTS OF LOVE: For Christmas

Ten days to go to Christmas now!!!

Today I sat for a little bit for the first time. Otherwise, I just slept as normal.

My nose is really sore and keeps bleeding. I am so, so scared.

***

DATE: 16.12.2003
WEATHER: Looks cold
WISH OF THE DAY: To get out of here for good
FAVOURITE FRIEND: Everyone
SPECIAL SECRET: I want to go home.
WHAT MAKES ME SAD: Being like this?
WHAT MAKES ME SMILE: It's all over.
THOUGHTS OF LOVE: For my family

Nine days to go till Christmas!!!

I can't wait to go home now. I'm fed up of being in here and hurting.

My eye is really sore, and my head really hurts.

I was told Tom is being good!!!

The news came that I might be able to go home the next day. I had an appointment at Hereford Hospital about my eye. I was going to have a temporary eye fitted whilst my final prosthetic eye was being finished.

We left the hospital the next morning, but I wasn't officially discharged. My bed kept open in case I was poorly and needed to go back. I didn't want to go back though. I was so sick on the way home. It was vile. So for the next twenty-four hours, the hospital remained on standby.

We arrived at Hereford County Hospital, and we into the Eign Suite. We went up to the reception, and I checked in for my appointment. We took a seat and waited in the waiting area.

A lovely-looking lady walked over to the area and called my name. She shook all of our hands, and we followed her down the corridor. She asked me about what had happened. We all explained. She asked what the hospital had done in the removal of my eye. And she removed the conformer, looked inside the socket, and said that it was healing nicely.

Leaning over toward a massive black box, she lifted the covering and pulled out all the draws. I found myself staring at rows and rows of eyes of different shapes, different thicknesses, and different colours. It was amazing. I bet she has had a fair few jokes cracked over that box.

The eye felt strange. It felt full. It was a bad match, and it was a different colour than was my real eye. My real eye is a hazel colour, and my new glass eye was a right green with a tiny pinprick pupil in the middle of it.

After the appointment, she showed us out. She explained that she would set me another appointment to have the moulds, wax copy, and photographs taken. That would enable her to make my new eye, which would be an exact match of my real one.

We went home. I was so pleased to see Tom. He was gentle as normal, and he just got it.

Christmas came around fast. I slept through most of it. Then New Year's came and went. I could only hope that 2004 would be a better year.

THE CSF LEAK: LUMBER DRAIN, LUMBER PUNCTURES, AND THE PLUG

Let your dreams be bigger *than your fears.*
Actions speak louder than words.
Faith is stronger than feelings.

Life pretty much went on the best that it could. I turned fourteen on the 6 January and went for another appointment with the solicitors. I was still getting sick and still having headaches – a lot.

It was so good. I travelled by train to an outpatient appointment at the Queen Elizabeth Hospital Birmingham to see the surgeon who had performed the last operation. He was pleased with me and the progress that I had made since the operation – so much so that he discharged me back into the care of the ear, nose, and throat specialist at Birmingham Children's Hospital.

I started back helping out in the toy shop.

I had gone back to school after Christmas as normal. And on Monday, 12 January 2004, was when it all started to happen. I was leaking. I was sitting down at the dining room table doing my homework when I first noticed it. My nose was dripping. Every time I put my head over to write, it was running. I told Mum and Dad. They were concerned and told me that they would ring the Birmingham doctor's secretary in the morning and ask for advice.

The doctor said I had to go back to the hospital and that I should get there as soon as I could. I arrived and found myself escorted to a bed on Ward 10. The doctor suspected I was having a CSF leak.

And so began the next fifteen long days:
- Day 1 – We travelled straight over. I leaked 4 millilitres of fluid from around my brain. I was to be watched for forty-eight hours to see if the leak would resolve itself.
- Day 2 – I was still leaking, but I was being watched. I had to collect the fluid to see how much I was losing.
- Day 3 – Yet again, I was still on Ward 10. The doctor hadn't yet decided what was to be done. Meanwhile, fluid was still leaking out of my right nostril.
- Day 4 – They had started to collect the fluid. They were going to compare the amounts on a day-to-day basis. In twelve hours, 5 millilitres of fluid was collected.
- Day 5 – Another 5 millilitres was collected in another twelve hours.
- Day 6 – The sixth day arrived, and I was still in. I had visitors, though, which was good for Mum. My auntie, uncle, and cousin came. It was so good to see people. More fluid was collected today – 7.8 millilitres in twelve hours. So they decided to put me to sleep and insert a lumboperitoneal drain.
- Day 7 – I leaked 3.4 millilitres of fluid before 1.00 p.m. So I went down to theatre. It was the fourth time

Claire Gale

I had been put to sleep by general anaesthesia. I was under for about an hour. The surgical team inserted a small flexible tube into my lumber spine. They hoped that it would stop the cerebrospinal fluid from leaking out of my nose via the hole created when the lead pellet had landed in my brain. I was transferred after the operation to Ward 9. I was placed on a special bed and kept at a certain position. When I look back to what happened next, I chuckle to myself. I was uncomfortable and in a lot of pain when I came round. All I wanted was my mum and dad. The nurses had explained that I couldn't move, well not suddenly at least because that could cause me to become paralysed. Dad tried to move the side of the bed down so that he could comfort me. Instead of pulling the side of the bed down, he pulled the emergency lever. What happened was something straight out of *Mr Bean*. The bed flew back straight down so I was flat on my back. Everyone panicked. The nurses ran straight down to my bed because the alarms were going off, and Mum and Dad had to move out whilst they propped me back up.

- Day 8 – I was still on Ward 9. The lumber drain, however, had not worked. Overnight, no CSF fluid had drained off, but it was still leaking from my nose. They collected 2.3 millilitres that day. The drain was removed. It felt strange. They just pulled the tube out of my spine. They then decided they were going to do lumber puncture instead.

- Day 9 – My doctors decided to wait another twenty-four hours before they put me through a lumber puncture. At the top of Ward 9, there was a procedure room. That's where the next procedure would be done. But the fluid leak was slowing, which was a good sign. At that point, I was hoping it wouldn't come to that.
- Day 10 – I had visitors that morning. My Auntie Pauline came. Then I had an eye appointment with the surgeon that had performed the operation to remove my eye so that she could check that everything was okay. I was wheeled down in a wheelchair, as I still wasn't able to walk. She was pleased with it.

    At 6.30 p.m., I was taken to the procedure room for the lumber puncture. It hurt so much. I cried loads, and Mum had to hold me still. The team drained off some fluid. After they had done it, I was wheeled back down to my bed, as again, I wasn't allowed to walk.

    Dad gave me a present for being brave. He bought me a tank with sea monkeys to make.

    That night, I dripped no more fluid.
- Day 11 – Still no CSF fluid was leaking. They were really pleased with me. They were going to hang fire on doing any more lumber punctures. Thank god. At 11.30 p.m., I was moved back over to Ward 10.
- Day 12 – I settled back into Ward 10. It was becoming like a second home. I knew all the nurses now, and I get on really well with everyone around me. There still wasn't any fluid leaking. The doctors were really pleased with what progress. They were talking about letting me home the next day.

- Day 13 – In the morning, I was sick. I was unsteady on my feet, and I was dizzy, both when I sat and when I stood. I still wasn't leaking fluid, but I still hadn't seen a doctor.
- Day 14 – I was discharged. Yippee. I had to agree, though, that I would go straight back if I have any more leaks. The journey home was terrible. I was incredibly sick. We had to keep stopping.
- Day 15 – I was home, but I slept till 1.00 p.m. I was so tired and drowsy.

On 30 January 2004, I started leaking CSF fluid from my nose again. The next day, Mum rung the hospital. I was advised to go to Birmingham Children's A & E, as I need to be admitted again. The hospital contacted the neurosurgeon, who was on standby for my arrival. Ward 9 was to prepare me a bed. My best friend wouldn't leave me. I had been through so much, and our friendship meant so much. She refused to stay at home with her family. She insisted that she wanted to come with me. So she did.

When we got to accident and emergency, we had a long wait. It took forever. The neurosurgeon wanted to be certain that I was leaking fluid. The team tried everything. They hung me upside down in a bed with my head hanging off the bed so that the fluid could drip onto the floor. That's when they realised it was dripping like it had before. So they moved me up onto the ward. My best friend had to leave, and Dad had to take her back.

On the Sunday, I finally saw my consultant at 9.30 p.m. He said that I would be having surgery the next day to insert a plug into my brain. He was going to be using fat from my body, he thought my earlobe, and he would be putting it up my nose to form a base for the hole. He arranged for me to have fluerascance injected into my spine at midday, so I'd be ready to go down to theatre at 2.00 p.m. Then he would be able to see exactly where the hole was.

From 7.00 a.m. the next morning, I wasn't allowed to eat. And I wasn't allowed to drink from 12.00 p.m. They wanted to perform a lumber puncture to insert the fluerascance into my spine. But the fluid never turned up. So my operation got postponed. The hospital rang round all the other hospitals to find some, but only the city hospital had any. The hospital was desperate for it, so they put a prescription up for it and sent it over to the city hospital. They then sent a taxi to collect it. The pharmaceutical team then had to declare it and dispatch it. Because the theatre was booked and all the team had been waiting for me, as soon as it arrived, they took me straight down to theatre. They performed the lumber puncture under general anaesthesia this time. Thank god. Lumber punctures hurt.

They thought the operation would take four hours, but after just two and a half hours, it was complete. And I was in recovery, ready to be moved back up to the ward.

I was sick when I came round; it was filled with blood. But the team was pleased with how the operation had gone. They thought I'd be in now for about a week. I had a stitch on my earlobe and a plaster on my nose. The doctor explained that he had done a procedure called a bath plug with a fate and mucosal graft. He explained to me in terms I could understand that, basically, he had taken the fat from my ear, put it in a piece of string, pushed it up my nose, and wrapped it around the hole. After he'd tied it right, he'd put glue over it and a piece of waterproof lining and then a bit more glue. He'd then pulled the string out the side of my nose and tied it tight to hold it in place – once and for all.

The next day I was discharged.

And – touch wood – that was the end of it. No more leaks.

Life just carried on, like *normal*.

Well, normal-ish.

FINDING MYSELF: 'NORMAL' LIFE

Sometimes I pretend
To be
Normal.
But then it gets boring.
So I
Go back
To being
Me.

Well, I'd love to tell you that life went back to normal. But, well, normal is boring. So I just continued to be me. Life bubbled along, and I adjusted. I had to, in ways that people will never get or understand. Life is different with one eye – especially when you were born and had thirteen years with two.

Emotions were flooding through and bubbling up, and I was holding them in. I was absorbing them and letting them consume me.

It would be nice to tell you that life was easy. But guess what? It wasn't. Life became hard – really hard. I wasn't sure if I was even meant to still be here; it sure didn't feel like it. I was sure that people thought I was a freak before, and now that I had one eye, they were going to think it even more. But I guess they didn't, and it just became normal. Whatever that is. It just became my life.

What people don't realise is your body is a wonderful thing, and it compensates automatically. So I was blind immediately, yet when I opened my eyes, it looked hardly different than it had in the first place. I can't remember what it's like to have two eyes – which pains me. I'd be lying if I told you I didn't miss it. I hated how this new eye looked, and yet I got told all the time it didn't look any different. It felt different, and when I looked in the mirror, it stood out like a sore thumb. It looked lazy. It looked false. And yeah, I may have trained it to move, but the movement was restricted because the arse did a bloody good job at what he did.

I know he probably didn't mean to. It was a freak accident, and he probably was hurting just as much as I was. But he walked away – with nothing wrong with him. He never apologised. He just hid from he had done, from life. An apology could have gone a long way. It wouldn't have turned back the hands of time, and it wouldn't have bought my eye back, but it may have helped – a little bit. It may have prevented me from carrying around all this pain and emotions I can't even describe for the past eleven years. It could have all been resolved long ago.

Life changed, though; everything changed. Living with monocular vision was different. I had a list of things I couldn't do. Because of the packing that had been inserted, I wasn't allowed to sneeze unless my mouth was open whilst I was on the ten-year watch. I can't go deep sea diving or scuba diving because of the pressure on my brain. I wasn't allowed to even blow my nose – a nightmare when you get a cold.

As life's routines started back up at school and stuff, I started to get panic attacks. Loud noises, shadows, and anything that reminded me of what had happened would cause them. Most people at the age of thirteen don't have skeletons in their closets. Yet I have a whole graveyard scaring me and holding me hostage – frozen in time to 16 October 2003.

I struggle with depth perception. It always sucks when I go to pour a drink, and I pour it all over the side of the glass. Or at times, I'll run the tap to get a glass of water and the water goes all up my sleeve because I put my hand too far under the tap, thinking it's farther back than it is.

I can't balance. I fall off curbs or trip up them, which hurts a lot. I can't see steps unless they have a reflective strip on them, which also can be awkward. There's no looking hot when you're stumbling to get up the stairs – one step at a time. I can't see escalators. They just look like ramps with the strips all going the same way. I'm forever holding the queue up to get on them to travel up or down. Would I go? Should I go? Oh, I've gone. And yay, I didn't trip.

I can't ride a bike. I get on the one side, and I fall off the other. Whoops. I don't seem to have much luck with bikes anyway, so it's probably for the best.

I can't see 3D, which sucks. I was hoping that it wouldn't take off, but now everything seems to be in 3D. With only one eye, my vision doesn't cross. So I can't pick the pictures up. It just looks blurry. I used to love those 3D books, where you put your nose right to the page and then you move it slowly back and focus in on the picture until suddenly the image jumps out at you. I still miss the little things. I guess I always will. I wish sometimes I'd never been shown the little things so that I wouldn't miss them now.

Fatigue often gets the better of me, and seems to be *a big* battle on a daily basis. I can't win. I either sleep my life away or battle through and put up with the consequences. I forget things a lot, and my life feels to be a big jumble of Post-it notes. I get the shopping, and because I feel like my life is on a loop and repeat, I always buy the same things – even if they're not needed. Baked beans and potatoes are a big one. I have cupboards of both. You'd think I'd learn and remember. But no. There is just something in my brain that tells me those items are needed. And you may say I should write a list. Well, that's a good idea. Now if I could just remember to take the shopping list with me and not leave it on the kitchen side. And even if I do take it, it's a piece of paper. I forget to look at it and think, *Ah, how hard can a spot of shopping be?*

I have alarms to remind me to do everything, and I have pieces of paper everywhere. I have to write lists, and I will keep rewriting them until they are perfect. I have certain colours for certain writing pads. It all gets a bit complicated. But in my head, that's the way it is. I look for perfection in everything. And yeah, I have the 'I-can't-be-arsed' approach. But when I get a burst of energy, everything has to be done, even if it means having no energy for a few days following and just sleeping.

I try my hardest to manage my energy, but even that gets tiring. I give up. I just carry on and do the best that I can with what I actually have. I do stupid things like pouring milk into gravy, not my coffee or putting the remote control in the fridge and lots of other little things.

Or if it's not that, it's my speech. My words come out all jumbled, and I sound stupid. Instead of getting my daughter a cardigan, I get her a pair of tights or ask her to put her school uniform on instead of her pyjamas. So then we end up just laughing at each other, with me laughing at myself and thinking, *Stupid cow*. Otherwise, I would cry. And crying doesn't solve anything. I say, 'Well, you know what I mean,' and carry on. What else can you do? Words get mixed up in sentences, and it all comes out in gobbledy gook. I give up!

But that's me now. That's my life, and these are the hurdles I face and deal with. The amount of times I have gone through this story, edited it, gotten people to read it, and checked that everything is in order is unbelievable.

Although there are lots of negative things and downsides associated with my situation, I also have a lot of fun. There are some good tricks you can play with a glass eye. Have you ever read *The Twits* by Roald Dahl? It gave me ideas.

'Will you watch my drink?' I'll ask as I slip my eye into my drink and leave it staring back up at the unsuspecting recipient of my joke. I froze my eye in ice cubes. When we had substitute teachers who didn't know me, they would ask, 'What are you doing?' My reply would be, 'Just cleaning my eye.' There I would be, sitting at the front of the class cleaning my eye on my tie. The sub would run out the room screaming.

French was always fun. The classroom was on a slant, and when I first had my eye, it wouldn't fit properly and fell out all the time.

'Miss?' I would say.

'Claire, in French?' the teacher would reply.

'I'm sorry,' I would say. 'I don't know how to say, "I sneezed, my eye fell out and rolled down the aisle, and it's now under the chalkboard." Can I come and get it?'

People's faces would always drop during these moments, and a smile would soon creep across my face.

My dad is squeamish, and because I had a couple of eyes, they would be left in draws or in the dining room. He always used to shout, 'Claire, can you come and get your eye?'

Mischievous, yes. But it's like they say. Every cloud has a silver lining, and being able to joke around was one of the things that got me used to my life with one eye. I wasn't scared of taking my eye out and freaking people out.

I must say I am better now and don't do it anymore – well, not as much. Over the last few years, I have finally found myself once again. I became happy. I have made friends, and I treasure them. And I once again treasure life. I hold onto the little things because they always mean the most. You should never give up on something small because it can often be the thing that means the most – a big thing.

So that's it. That's me – all laid bare for you all to read about.

I may be shaped differently from everyone else around here, but I'm me. And I'm proud of who I've become. I treasure what I have left in my life, as it means so much to me.

Things work in mysterious ways. There isn't a correct answer for anything. You just have to try your best to succeed.

But now you all know all the hurt and pain and struggles I went through. You know what I have dealt with and overcome, the challenges I continue to deal with, and how I cope on a daily basis.

How would you have done it? Would you have done it differently than I did? Would you still be here standing tall and fighting? Or would you have given up long ago?

I may not be perfect. I may have a hole in me, and I may be a bit battered around the edges. But you know something – just try and make the best out of every situation. I always have. I have done so from that moment when my life changed.

And I always will.

***

PS. This is a not for *you*.
I owe you *nothing* but want to thank you.
Without this weakness you gave me,
I wouldn't have realised how strong I actually can be.

***

Never be ashamed of scars. They just prove that you are stronger than what ever tried to hurt you!

***

A word to the wise –

Good luck and just remember this is the end …

Well for now anyway!

Printed in Great Britain
by Amazon